4

# A New Kind of Faith

Participant's Guide

**Other Resources by Lee Strobel**

*The Case for Christ*
*The Case for Christ* audio
*The Case for Christ—Student Edition* (with Jane Vogel)
*The Case for Christmas*
*The Case for a Creator*
*The Case for a Creator* audio
*The Case for Creator—Student Edition* (with Jane Vogel)
*The Case for Easter*
*The Case for Faith*
*The Case for Faith* audio
*The Case for Faith—Student Edition* (with Jane Vogel)
*Experiencing the Passion of Jesus* (with Garry Poole)
*God's Outrageous Claims*
*Inside the Mind of Unchurched Harry and Mary*
*Surviving a Spiritual Mismatch in Marriage*
     (with Leslie Strobel)
*Surviving a Spiritual Mismatch in Marriage* audio
*What Jesus Would Say*

**Other Resources by Garry Poole**

*The Complete Book of Questions*
*Seeker Small Groups*
*The Three Habits of Highly Contagious Christians*
**In the Tough Questions Series:**
*Don't All Religions Lead to God?*
*How Could God Allow Suffering and Evil?*
*How Does Anyone Know God Exists?*
*Why Become a Christian?*
*Tough Questions Leader's Guide* (with Judson Poling)

**4**

# A New Kind of Faith

Participant's Guide

Four Sessions on the Relevance of Christianity

# Lee Strobel and Garry Poole

ZONDERVAN™

GRAND RAPIDS, MICHIGAN 49530 USA

WILLOW

Willow Creek Resources

ZONDERVAN.COM/
AUTHORTRACKER

**ZONDERVAN**™

*A New Kind of Faith Participant's Guide*
Copyright © 2006 by Lee Strobel and Rocket Pictures

Requests for information should be addressed to:

Zondervan, *Grand Rapids, Michigan 49530*

ISBN-10: 0-310-26860-5

ISBN-13: 978-0-310-26860-4

*Interior design by Angela Moulter*

*Printed in the United States of America*

06  07  08  09  10  11  12  •  10  9  8  7  6  5  4  3  2  1

# Contents

*Special thanks to Ann Kroeker and Laura Allen*
*for their outstanding writing and editing contributions.*
*Their creative insights and suggestions*
*took these guides to the next level.*

# Preface

The idea came to me in the shower one morning: why not create a television program in which people of various beliefs—from Muslims to Christians to atheists to New Agers—could debate the most provocative spiritual and moral issues of the day?

What's more, prominent religious leaders could be invited on the program to be cross-examined about the stickiest questions concerning their faith.

Thanks to the vision and creativity of Jim Berger and Joni Holder, we ended up producing *Faith Under Fire*™ for a national television network. As predicted, the weekly show generated a slew of vociferous letters from viewers around the country. More than one person admitted that he found himself shouting back at his TV set.

This curriculum is based on the interviews and debates we aired on the program. You'll see knowledgeable and passionate experts discussing not just *what* they believe, but *why* they believe it. Our hope is that your group will provide a safe environment for you to be able to share your own thoughts and opinions—as well as to consider the viewpoints of others.

You'll quickly see that many of the claims made by the experts are mutually exclusive. In other words, the Christian and Muslim cannot both be right if the Bible claims Jesus is the Son of God and the Koran asserts that he's not divine but merely a prophet. One of them might be correct, or both of them could be in error, but each one of them cannot be true at the same time.

That's why we insist that our experts back up their claims. Can they defend their position logically? Do they have evidence from history or science that supports their assertions? Our task should be to determine where the evidence points.

In a similar way, the U.S. Constitution provides equal protection to all expressions of faith, and yet that doesn't mean all religious claims are equally true. According to the U.S. Supreme Court, the American ideal is to create a "marketplace of ideas" in which various opinions and beliefs can freely battle with each other so that truth will ultimately prevail.

So what is "true" about God, about Jesus, and about the afterlife? What can we know with confidence about issues of faith and morality? I hope you'll grapple with these issues in unhindered debate and discussion in your group.

One thing is true for sure: a lot hinges on the outcome.

*Lee Strobel*

SESSION
1

# Must
# Christianity
# Change
# or Die?

# Read It!

*Reality Check?*

Galileo Galilei held to some radical ideas that ran contrary to church doctrine in the 1600s. Get this: This guy actually claimed that the *Sun*, not the Earth, was at the center of the solar system. Can you believe that? Of course you can! By now that's scientifically proven and astronomically accurate. That fact is so obvious that it seems ludicrous the church would have ever had a problem with it.

But it did.

Galileo was taken to trial by the church authorities for these "outlandish" beliefs. Theology of that time hinged on the assumed reality that the Earth was the center of the universe. As far as the church was concerned, Galileo's claim messed up its entire belief system.

The first time he was brought to trial, he was found innocent and warned not to teach the Copernican, Sun-centered system ever again. Later, with permission from the church under the leadership of a new pope, Galileo published a book presenting a creative dialogue between friends—the most brilliant friend took the Sun-centered point of view, while the simpleminded character represented the Earth-centered view. It was supposed to present these ideas as theory, but the book made it obvious who was right and who was the idiot.

The church didn't like this book. The pope, suspecting he was a model for the simpleminded character, halted the book's printing and put Galileo, then sixty-eight, on trial for teaching the Copernican theory after being ordered not to.

When threatened with torture, Galileo publicly confessed that he had been wrong to have said that the Earth moved around the Sun. He was found guilty and sentenced to life imprisonment. Because of his age and fame, they adapted the imprisonment to house arrest, where Galileo Galilei lived out the final years of his life.

Oh, but the church came around. In 1992 Pope John Paul II publicly endorsed a papal commission's finding that the church had made a mistake in condemning Galileo.

Wait—did you catch the year?—1992! It only took the church *350 years* to admit the truth and face reality. That's a snail's pace approach to change, wouldn't you say? Shouldn't Christianity evolve more efficiently than that?

If you're not careful, you'd think God invaded the earth through the miracle of the virgin birth and then escaped the earth through the miracle of the cosmic ascension. Or would you? Aren't those just weak, first-century attempts to try to make sense out of a few unusual events?

The church claims it's reality, but is it *really* reality?

The idea that somehow the blood of Jesus is necessary to cleanse people from their sins draws on concepts that are just plain unbelievable. That God would work out salvation by killing his own Son appears to be some kind of an act of divine child abuse.

The church maintains the Bible is the inerrant word of God, yet it seems to pick and choose which commands to follow and which to ignore. For example, many churches teach from the Old Testament that Christians should tithe, yet no one is following the Old Testament commandment to stone sons for disobeying their parents.

The church seems stuck on claims made in the first century or even before. Isn't it time for the church to fully embrace a new day and age? We need a bold, life-changing faith that can take us confidently into the future.

Can Christianity do that? Can it get a makeover? Now's as good a time as any.

## Watch It!

Use the following space to take notes as you view the video in which Lee Strobel interviews retired Episcopal bishop John Shelby Spong, the controversial author of *Christianity Must Change or Die*, and Dr. Albert Mohler, president of Southern Baptist Theological Seminary, and according to Time.com, the reigning intellectual of the evangelical movement in the United States.

# Discuss It!

*1* To what extent is Christianity outdated? Under what circumstances could a 2,000-year-old religion still be relevant?

*2* Bishop Spong believes that Christianity needs to be updated because we live on the other side of Galileo, Darwin, and Einstein. Do you agree that the historical records of Jesus' miracles, teachings, and resurrection should be discarded in favor of a religion devoid of the traditional teachings of the church? Why or why not?

*3* Spong does not believe that "God decided to invade the earth through the miracle of the virgin birth and then escape the earth through the miracle of the cosmic ascension." Do you agree or disagree with Spong? Explain.

> "I do not feel obliged to believe that the same God who has endowed us with sense, reason and intellect has intended us to forgo their use."
>
> **Galileo**

**4** Spong says, "I'm really not interested in a God who works out salvation by killing the Son of God. I find that to be an act of divine child abuse." On the other hand, Dr. Mohler points out that the Bible clearly teaches the substitutionary atonement—that Jesus willingly went to the cross to pay the penalty for our wrong-doing so that we can be reconciled with God if we choose. How do you respond to these very different viewpoints?

**5** Do you agree with Bishop Spong's statement that "it is only those people who believe they possess the truth that want to have inquisitions, do heresy hunts, start wars, or persecute people who disagree with them"? Why or why not? Jesus, who says he *is* truth, tells his followers to be loving toward others. Is it possible to believe in truth and yet still be compassionate and caring toward people with different opinions?

**6** "Nobody possesses the truth." Do you agree or disagree with this statement? Explain your response. To what extent do you think we can know and understand the truth about God?

## Watch It!

Use the following space to take notes as Lee Strobel continues to interview John Shelby Spong and Dr. Albert Mohler.

## Discuss It!

**7** Albert Mohler states, "If we can't know the truth about God, we're lost in the universe." To what extent do you agree or disagree with this statement?

**8** Read the Bible verses listed below along with the corresponding summary statements of several common beliefs of the Christian faith. Which statements do you agree with, and which ones do you disagree with? Which beliefs, if any, do you think are essential or indispensable to the teachings of Christianity? Which are not? Give reasons for your responses.

**There is one God, eternally existing in three persons: Father, Son, and Holy Spirit.**

> "Don't you believe that I am in the Father, and that the Father is in me? The words I say to you are not just my own. Rather, it is the Father, living in me, who is doing his work.... But the Counselor, the Holy Spirit, whom the Father will send in my name, will teach you all things and will remind you of everything I have said to you." (John 14:10, 26)

> "When the Counselor comes, whom I will send to you from the Father, the Spirit of truth who goes out from the Father, he will testify about me." (John 15:26)

**The Bible is the inspired, infallible, authoritative Word of God.**

> All Scripture is God-breathed and is useful for teaching, rebuking, correcting and training in righteousness. (2 Timothy 3:16)

**Jesus Christ, conceived by the Holy Spirit, was born of the Virgin Mary, and was true God and true man, existing in one person and without sin.**

> *In the beginning was the Word, and the Word was with God, and the Word was God. He was with God in the beginning. Through him all things were made; without him nothing was made that has been made.... He was in the world, and though the world was made through him, the world did not recognize him.... The Word became flesh and made his dwelling among us. (John 1:1–3, 10, 14)*

> *[Jesus said,] "I and the Father are one." (John 10:30)*

> *Therefore the Lord himself will give you a sign: The virgin will be with child and will give birth to a son. (Isaiah 7:14)*

**All human beings are born with a sinful nature that leads them to sin in thought, word, and deed.**

> *For all have sinned and fall short of the glory of God. (Romans 3:23)*

**Jesus' crucifixion, death, burial, and bodily resurrection atones for the sins of humankind.**

> *This man [Jesus] was handed over to you by God's set purpose and foreknowledge; and you, with the help of wicked men, put him to death by nailing him to the cross. But God raised him from the dead, freeing him from the agony of death, because it was impossible for death to keep its hold on him. (Acts 2:23–24)*

> *But God demonstrates his own love for us in this: While we were still sinners, Christ died for us. (Romans 5:8)*

Salvation, an unearned gift of forgiveness of all one's sins, is given to anyone who believes in and receives Jesus Christ by faith.

*For it is by grace you have been saved, through faith — and this not from yourselves, it is the gift of God — not by works, so that no one can boast. (Ephesians 2:8 – 9)*

*Know that a man is not justified by observing the law, but by faith in Jesus Christ. So we, too, have put our faith in Christ Jesus that we may be justified by faith in Christ and not by observing the law, because by observing the law no one will be justified. (Galatians 2:16)*

*Jesus answered, "I am the way and the truth and the life. No one comes to the Father except through me." (John 14:6)*

*For the wages of sin is death, but the gift of God is eternal life in Christ Jesus our Lord. (Romans 6:23)*

*For God did not send his Son into the world to condemn the world, but to save the world through him. Whoever believes in him is not condemned, but whoever does not believe stands condemned already because he has not believed in the name of God's one and only Son. (John 3:17 – 18)*

**9** Which authority holds more weight for you: the authority of the Bible (which claims to be God's Word) or the authority of modern knowledge? Is it possible that the two are not contradictory, but that a careful examination of scientific and historical evidence might support the historic reliability of the Bible? Explain why you place your faith where you do.

**10** Spong claims that "no human being can know the reality of God." He suggests that religious explanations "are all human attempts to minister to human security needs to believe that we possess the truth." Explain what you think Spong means and why you agree or disagree with him.

**11** Dr. Mohler argues that the heart of Christianity—as taught in all four Gospels and throughout the New Testament, as well as prophesied of in the Old Testament—is that Christ died in our place and paid the price of our sins. What reasons do you have for agreeing or disagreeing with Mohler's argument?

# 12 In what ways should Christianity change? In what ways should it stay the same?

## Watch It!  *Lee's Perspective*

I don't think Bishop Spong could be more wrong. The most compelling scholarship today, both in the scientific and historical realms, points toward the truth of Christianity as taught by those who were closest to the scene—that is, the authors of the New Testament. The scientific theories and discoveries of Galileo, Darwin, and Einstein don't negate the truth of Scripture. Rather, the essential claims of Christianity are more supported today than ever before.

To Spong, the supernatural events of the New Testament are impossible, and therefore the virgin birth, the miracles of Jesus, and the resurrection must be mythological. Personally, I think it's more logical to draw conclusions based on the evidence—and I'm convinced that the evidence of science and history support the reliability of Christianity's traditional beliefs.

Let's not believe in the authority of the Bible merely because the Bible claims to be true. Let's look at modern cosmology, physics, biochemistry, and genetics, all of which point powerfully toward a supernatural Creator who looks suspiciously like the God of the Bible. Let's examine the evidence of archaeology, the fulfillment of Old Testament prophecies against all mathematical odds, the eyewitness accounts, and the corroboration by outside sources that all support the reliability of the Bible. Based on all of this, I believe it's logical and rational to believe in the claims of the Christian Scriptures.

Must Christianity change? Of course, its methodology needs to be updated for every generation. For instance, the language it employs must keep abreast of the changing culture, and churches must meet modern needs that were unknown to Jesus' disciples. But to change Christianity's message—especially such central elements as the atonement and resurrection—is to gut the faith of all its meaning. And that is simply not warranted by the facts.

## Chart It!

At this point in your spiritual journey, what do you believe about the Christian faith? On a scale from one to ten, place an X near the spot and phrase that best describes you. Share your selection with the rest of the group and give reasons for placing your X where you did.

| 1 | 2 | 3 | 4 | 5 | 6 | 7 | 8 | 9 | 10 |
|---|---|---|---|---|---|---|---|---|---|
| I'm not convinced the Christian faith is relevant and true. | | | | I'm unsure what to believe about the Christian faith. | | | | I'm convinced the Christian faith is relevant and true. | |

## Study It!

Take some time later this week to check out what the Bible teaches about the reliability of its Scriptures.

+ John 3
+ Romans 5
+ Ephesians 2

# The End
## of Faith?

## Read It!

*Fantasy World?*

Just before her husband turned off the late-night newscast, Janice rolled over and mumbled, "I'm so tired of hearing about wars and abuse and all those victims." Her husband asked what she said, but she was just entering that zone between waking and sleeping. He didn't even hear her last question. It sounded more like a sigh: "Wouldn't it be nice if everyone could just get along?"

She slept late the next morning and shuffled to the mailbox in her slippers. She picked up the paper and saw her neighbor Pete waving the hedge clippers in the air, like an extended arm. "Hi, Janice! Beautiful morning, isn't it?"

Still groggy, Janice waved her paper in the same way. "I'll find out once I read this and get my morning coffee!" As she spoke, however, something seemed strange about the interaction.

"Let me know if you'd like me to trim that boxwood for you. I'd be happy to while I have my clippers out."

"Okay, I'll think about it and let you know," Janice answered, a puzzled look on her face.

"Great! I'd just go ahead and do it, but I'd want to be sure to shape it the way you want. I'll check with you later," he called back to her. "Good to see you, Janice—have a great day!"

As he turned back to snip his shrubs, Janice thought, *Strange. He's so pleasant and sincere. What's up with that?*

A few moments later, as she stirred the cream in her first cup of coffee, she realized it was Sunday morning. *Sunday morning? Pete and his family are always at church on a Sunday! That's what's strange—not only is it odd for him to be home, but he was actually doing some chores and offering to do more!* She pondered this as she took a sip of coffee and pulled the plastic bag off the newspaper. *That guy's so religious, he'd never do chores on a Sunday. Besides, he usually makes me feel guilty for not being a churchgoer. Maybe they had a problem at their church. People are always having problems with their churches.*

She laid the front page open and glanced at the story about Ireland. It was about peace. The photo showed some Irish men and women drinking a toast to friendship and unity, Northern and Southern Ireland were one united country, free from strife.

Baffled at such a sudden change, she turned the page — Israel's prime minister was shaking hands with the leader of the Palestinians. The story stated that the two leaders are actively working on how they'll share the land.

"What's going on here?" Janice said out loud. "What happened overnight? It's all about peace, people getting along, disagreements disappearing. What's the deal?"

She turned on the TV. The newscaster was saying, "Crime is at an all-time low. Surveys conducted throughout the nation reveal that people feel that the world is a more peaceful place to live than ever before. They feel safer, and in a unique survey conducted in major metropolitan areas such as New York City and Los Angeles, people were asked about how free they feel to share their belongings. Seventy-seven percent of the respondents expressed that they were very comfortable sharing with neighbors."

Janice rubbed her eyes. "What is this? Some kind of a joke?"

She flipped the channels and found an interview with the Secretary of State. "Things being as they are, terrorism has become practically a non-issue."

"What?" Janice exclaimed. "What's happening?"

As she flipped through more channels, some were missing, simply static. She tried to remember what those channels were. Then it dawned on her: those are the religious channels.

She phoned her husband, who was working over the weekend at the office. "Honey, what in the world is happening? There's peace between nations that have always been at war, everyone's talking about getting along, befriending each other. And then there's this weird thing here at home—the religious channels on TV are all static."

Her husband was silent for a moment. "Are you okay, sweetheart?"

"What do you mean, am *I* okay?"

"You're not making sense," he said calmly.

"Nothing's making sense!"

"Relax, honey. I'm just wondering if you're okay because I don't know what you mean. You're using some words I've never heard before, so I just ..."

"Words you've never ... what? What words?"

"You said something, but it didn't make sense to me. About the TV."

"Yes, the religious channels are all static."

"That's it—'religious.' I don't know what you mean."

"Religion, you know, the religious fanatics preaching and quoting the Bible."

There was a long silence on the other end of the phone. "What you said—those words, those concepts. You sound like you're speaking English, but I've never heard of those things."

Janice hung up the phone without even saying good-bye. She pulled out the newspaper again, and then realized what was missing: religion. She figured out an explanation for this fantasy world she woke up in. There was not one word about religious differences, only an abundance of stories about peace and generosity, people working together to solve their problems.

It seems that religion is indeed gone, wiped out, or maybe it never existed at all ... and the world is a better place.

"So that was the real problem," Janice muttered. "Religion was the problem all along."

A loud buzzer sounded and Janice got up to check the dryer. She hit the knob, but it kept buzzing. She slapped it harder, then looked up to see it was the alarm clock going off.

"I'm headed off to work today, honey," her husband whispered. "Sorry to do this on a Sunday."

## Watch It!

Use the following space to take notes as you view the video in which Lee Strobel interviews Sam Harris, author of *End of Faith*, and Hugh Hewitt, a nationally syndicated radio host and author of several books, including, *If It's Not Close, They Can't Cheat.*

# Discuss It!

**1** Do you believe that faith is irrational? Why or why not?

**2** Define *fanatic*. Are all religious people fanatics? Are all fanatics religious? Explain.

**3** Give an example of religious fanaticism. Is it possible to be a sincere, fully devoted follower of a religion without being fanatical? Explain.

**4** To what extent do you think evil is done in the name of faith? Explain. What are some examples of positive things done in the name of religion?

**5** True or False: Religion taken to its logical end inevitably leads to war and terrorism. Explain.

**6** If some religious faiths justify certain forms of cruelty, should any religious faith be tolerated at all? Explain.

## Watch It!

Use the following space to take notes as Lee Strobel continues to interview Sam Harris and Hugh Hewitt.

## Discuss It!

**7** Given the negative results of religion, do you think our world would be a better place without religious faith? Explain. If all religion and faith in God were suppressed, would violence and war cease to exist? Why or why not?

**8** Do you believe it is ethical to use violence to eliminate religious violence? Are there ever any circumstances when faith justifies cruelty? Explain.

**9** Sam Harris makes the argument that the Christian belief that God sends non-Christians to hell makes it logically impossible for Christians to respect the beliefs of non-Christians. Do you agree or disagree? Explain.

# 10 What do the following Bible verses teach regarding evil?

*"This is the verdict: Light has come into the world, but men loved darkness instead of light because their deeds were evil." (John 3:19)*

*There is no one who understands, no one who seeks God. (Romans 3:11)*

*Seek good, not evil, that you may live. (Amos 5:14)*

*Love must be sincere. Hate what is evil; cling to what is good.... Do not repay anyone evil for evil.... Do not be overcome by evil, but overcome evil with good. (Romans 12:9, 17, 21)*

*"The thief [Satan] comes only to steal and kill and destroy; I [Jesus] have come that they may have life, and have it to the full." (John 10:10)*

*"You belong to your father, the devil, and you want to carry out your father's desire. He was a murderer from the beginning, not holding to the truth, for there is no truth in him. When he lies, he speaks his native language, for he is a liar and the father of lies." (John 8:44)*

*Then I saw a new heaven and a new earth, for the first heaven and the first earth had passed away.... And I heard a loud voice from the throne saying, "Now the dwelling of God is with men, and he will live with them. They will be his people, and God himself will be with them and be their God. He will wipe every tear from their eyes. There will be no more death or mourning or crying or pain, for the old order of things has passed away." He who was seated on the throne said, "I am making everything new!" (Revelation 21:1, 3–5)*

**11** Do you think religion causes people to commit evil or do people who commit evil use religion as an excuse to justify their actions?

**12** Sam Harris contends that "the madman can find justification for his beliefs in almost any of our Scriptures." If Scripture were not available, to what extent would that prevent the madman from committing his madness?

**13** Hugh Hewitt believes religions go bad because people are bad. Do you agree or disagree with his line of reasoning? Explain.

**Watch It!** *Lee's Perspective*

Some critics agree with Sam Harris that faith is irrational. "The whole point of faith," said Michael Shermer, editor of *Skeptic* magazine, "is to believe regardless of the evidence, which is the very antithesis of science."

I disagree. To me, faith is a step we take in the *same direction* the evidence is pointing. And I've written books totaling more than a thousand pages in which I've described the evidence from science and history that convinced me—as an atheist—that Jesus is the unique Son of God who established his identity by rising from the dead. Consequently, following his teachings makes all the sense in the world to me.

It's true that Jesus teaches that he is the way, the truth, and the life, and that he's the sole path to the Father. At the same time, he instructs his followers to love and sacrificially serve others, as he first served us. I don't see these teachings as being incompatible. In fact, it was because of his great love for the entire world that Jesus chose to pay for our sins on the cross so that we can be reconciled with God through him.

Harris is simply wrong. Following the Prince of Peace does not inevitably lead to conflict and war. While it's true that imperfect people have seized on Scripture to justify violence and hatred, they were clearly not following the path set forth by Jesus himself. And they were a small minority. Think of all the positive ways that Christians have contributed to societies through the centuries—from the building of schools and hospitals to serving the poor and campaigning for social justice. They were motivated by the teachings of Jesus to help the least among us.

"Both Aristotle and Plato held that most humans are by nature slavish and suitable only for slavery," Michael Novak wrote. "Most do not have natures worthy of freedom. The Greeks used 'dignity' for only the few, rather than for all human beings. By contrast, Christianity insisted that every single human is loved by the Creator, made in the Creator's image, and destined for eternal friendship and communion with him."

Harris is looking in the wrong place. It wasn't Christianity but atheism that led to the deaths of more than a hundred million people in the last century. I agree with evangelist Luis Palau: "Humanity has paid a steep, gruesome price for the awful experiments in deliberate antitheism carried out by Lenin, Hitler, Stalin, Mao Tse-tung and others—each of whom was profoundly influenced by the writings of the apostles of atheism. After watching atheism proliferate ... it's clearer than ever that ... without God, we're lost."

## Chart It!

At this point in your spiritual journey, what do you believe about religion and evil? On a scale from one to ten, place an X near the spot and phrase that best describes you. Share your selection with the rest of the group and give reasons for placing your X where you did.

| 1 | 2 | 3 | 4 | 5 | 6 | 7 | 8 | 9 | 10 |
|---|---|---|---|---|---|---|---|---|---|
| I'm not convinced that religious faith results in more good than harm. | | | | I'm unsure how religious faith impacts our world. | | | | I'm convinced that religious faith results in more good than harm. | |

## Study It!

Take some time later this week to check out what the Bible teaches about the reliability of its Scriptures.

+ John 8
+ 2 Thessalonians 2:1–10
+ Revelation 21:1–7

SESSION
3

# Time for
# a *New God?*

# Read It!

*No Differences?*

Ted and Tom are neighbors who live in similar looking houses on the same side of the street and drive similar cars to the same jobsite, an industrial plant on the other side of town.

They started meeting for breakfast on Thursdays before carpooling to work.

"I can't believe how much we have in common," Tom said as they found a table.

"I only wish we started this tradition earlier," Ted agreed. "How long has it been since you moved into the neighborhood?"

"About a year," Tom answered.

"I can't believe that for the last year, all we did was wave when our garage doors opened or closed."

"Speaking of that, I couldn't help but notice that you and your family leave about the same time as we do on Sunday mornings. You a churchgoing man?"

"I am," Ted responded. "You too?"

"I am! How about that!" Tom exclaimed. "It's so amazing to find yet another thing in common."

"I know. It's nice to know we share so many interests, especially something as important as faith."

They were silent for a moment while they finished off their meals. "Isn't it great that God is so forgiving?" Tom offered rhetorically. "That's what drew me to him in the first place."

Ted pulled off the plastic lid to let his coffee cool. "I don't know," he began, "I always found comfort in knowing that God is a perfect judge who will wipe out all the evil in the world."

"Well, okay," Tom conceded, "I can see that. He's both forgiving *and* judging."

"We need God to judge people because they are basically evil," Ted stated firmly.

Tom absently stirred his coffee a moment. "People may do evil things, but they're basically good."

"Really?" Ted responded. "Where do you get that?"

"That's what I believe."

"I form my beliefs on the Bible," Ted said. "Every word of it is God's Word."

"Sure, the Bible is from God—for the most part—but there are some outdated parts in there. Parts of it really ought to be toned down. I mean, come on, Ted. All that stuff about hell?"

"Hell? Hell is designed specifically for evil people!"

"I only believe in heaven."

"How does *that* work?" Ted challenged.

"Simple," Tom explained, "evil people are reincarnated and given another chance. There's no need for hell."

"So what do you believe about Jesus?" Ted asked.

"What do you mean?"

"Well, do you believe he was God?"

"Well, he was definitely a good teacher, but I doubt whether he was actually God," Tom said.

"I agree that Jesus was a good teacher, absolutely. But to me, Jesus was God."

Tom smiled, "That's fine. Looks like we don't agree on all the details here, but that doesn't bother me one bit. You're just taking that path, it seems."

"That path?"

"That path to God. Jesus seems to be a good path for you to get to God," Tom suggested.

"Hey, I think he's the *only* path to God," Ted claimed.

"I think he's *a* path to God—a good one even. And I'm on that path myself, although there are so many others that work well."

"We *do* have some differences."

"But not many."

"I suppose," Ted conceded. "We still have so much in common, even our beliefs. Maybe the differences don't really matter too much."

"I don't think they do, Ted."

Ted finished his last drop of coffee before suggesting, "It's nice to know we share the same faith ..."

" ... the same beliefs ..." Tom offered.

" ... in the same God," Ted concluded.

# Watch It!

Use the following space to take notes as you view the video in which Lee Strobel interviews Irwin Kula, an eighth-generation rabbi who says the God of his fathers is not the right God for this age and that it's time for a new God, and Mark Mittelberg, a Christian speaker and author of the book *Building a Contagious Church*, who says God is knowable and unchanging.

## Discuss It!

**1** Is God knowable? To what extent do we have the capacity to understand or to know the truth about God?

**2** Mark Mittelberg believes that God is eternal and unchanging as revealed in the Old and New Testaments. He also believes we can know God personally. Who is God to you? Do you believe we can know God personally? Why or why not?

**3** Irwin Kula believes that all of us have some fragment of the total truth of God's reality even if that's only a one-percent fragment. Mittelberg argues that people harbor a lot of false ideas about God. What problem, if any, do these different viewpoints pose for you? Explain your answer.

**4** Is God *objective* in terms of his reality? In other words, do you believe there are some beliefs about God that are true and some that are false, or is everyone's *subjective* definition of God equally valid?

**5** What is significant about the difference between what people might imagine, project, or hope God is like and what the real God has revealed himself to be?

## Watch It!

Use the following space to take notes as Lee Strobel continues to interview Irwin Kula and Mark Mittelberg.

## Discuss It!

**6** Consider the following belief systems:

- There is one God (Christianity and Judaism).
- There is no God (Buddhism).
- There are many gods (Hinduism).

Can each of these belief systems all be true at the same time? Why or why not? Is the truth about God logical and consistent to all groups of people or is it contradictory to different groups of people? Explain.

**7** Do you believe that two contradictory beliefs cannot both be true at the same time? Why or why not?

> "There is a relationship between mystery and contradiction that easily reduces us to confusing the two. We do not understand mysteries. We cannot understand contradictions. The point of contact between the two concepts is their unintelligible character.... Further light may resolve present mysteries. However, there is not enough light in heaven and earth to ever resolve a clear-cut contradiction."
>
> **R. C. Sproul,** *Essential Truths of the Christian Faith*

**8** Do you believe it would greatly defuse religious tension if we could simply say everyone's got a piece of the truth and everyone's basically right in his or her own way? Why or why not?

**9** Mittelberg believes that if every religion were valid, God would be schizophrenic. Kula argues that God, being infinite, can hold together as true what we, being finite, may see as contradictions. Which argument do you agree with most? Explain your thinking.

> "Can you fathom the mysteries of God? Can you probe the limits of the Almighty?"
>
> **Job 11:7**

**10** At this point in your spiritual journey, what do you believe about the nature of God? According to the Bible verses listed here and on page 48, what does God reveal about himself? With which statements do you agree and which ones do you disagree? Give reasons for your responses.

## God is one.

*Hear, O Israel: The LORD our God, the LORD is one. (Deuteronomy 6:4)*

*Acknowledge and take to heart this day that the LORD is God in heaven above and on the earth below. There is no other. (Deuteronomy 4:39)*

## God is omnipotent.

*Praise him for his acts of power; praise him for his surpassing greatness. (Psalm 150:2)*

*"I am the LORD, the God of all mankind. Is anything too hard for me?" (Jeremiah 32:27)*

*Do you not know? Have you not heard? The LORD is the everlasting God, the Creator of the ends of the earth. He will not grow tired or weary, and his understanding no one can fathom. (Isaiah 40:28)*

## God is omnipresent.

*"Can anyone hide in secret places so that I cannot see him?" declares the LORD. "Do not I fill heaven and earth?" declares the LORD. (Jeremiah 23:24)*

## God is omniscient.

*Nothing in all creation is hidden from God's sight. Everything is uncovered and laid bare before the eyes of him to whom we must give account. (Hebrews 4:13)*

*Great is our Lord and mighty in power; his understanding has no limit. (Psalm 147:5)*

## God is eternal.

*The eternal God is your refuge, and underneath are the everlasting arms. (Deuteronomy 33:27)*

*He said to me: "It is done. I am the Alpha and the Omega, the Beginning and the End. To him who is thirsty I will give to drink without cost from the spring of the water of life." (Revelation 21:6)*

## God is truth.

*Into your hands I commit my spirit; redeem me, O Lord, the God of truth. (Psalm 31:5)*

*For God is not a God of disorder but of peace. (1 Corinthians 14:33)*

## God is unchanging.

*Jesus Christ is the same yesterday and today and forever. (Hebrews 13:8)*

## God is love.

*Give thanks to the God of gods. His love endures forever. (Psalm 136:2)*

*Whoever does not love does not know God, because God is love. (1 John 4:8)*

> " 'For my thoughts are not your thoughts, neither are your ways my ways,' declares the Lord. 'As the heavens are higher than the earth, so are my ways higher than your ways and my thoughts than your thoughts.' "
>
> **Isaiah 55:8 – 9**

**11** To what extent do you believe that God has resisted our attempts to define him but has instead objectively defined and revealed himself?

**12** How do you determine what's true and what's not true about God?

## Watch It! *Lee's Perspective*

I agree with Irwin Kula that we cannot know everything about God. But I also agree with Mark Mittelberg: we *can* know *some* things with confidence, particularly what God has chosen to reveal to us. In fact, God has told us all we need to know in order to relate to him.

God cannot be a personal being and an impersonal force at the same time. He cannot be existent and nonexistent at the same time. He cannot be many and one at the same time. He cannot be part of creation and separate from creation at the same time. As Mittelberg said, this would make God schizophrenic. Therefore, some beliefs that people have about God are true and others must be false.

For instance, Christianity claims Jesus is the Son of God. Islam explicitly says God doesn't have a son. Both claims cannot be true at the same time. It seems to me that our task, if we're seeking after truth, is to investigate where the evidence points. Which belief is best supported by logic, science, and history?

As I delved into ancient history as a spiritual skeptic, I became convinced of the reliability of the New Testament, that Jesus did teach that he was the Son of God, and that he authenticated that claim through his resurrection from the dead. So it seemed logical and rational for me to become a follower of Jesus.

Yes, I believe we all should be humble concerning our faith. Yes, I believe we should be tolerant and loving toward people of all beliefs. But let's not kid ourselves: all religions aren't saying the same thing about God and therefore all faiths cannot be true at the same time. At the foundational level, the world religions contradict each other.

That's why our approach on *Faith Under Fire* has been to focus not merely on *what* people believe, but *why* they believe it. Does it make sense? Is it defensible? How do you know it's true?

In fact, let me ask you this: how would you answer those questions based on what *you* believe?

## Chart It!

At this point in your spiritual journey, what do you believe about God and truth? On a scale from one to ten, place an X near the spot and phrase that best describes you. Share your selection with the rest of the group and give reasons for placing your X where you did.

| 1 | 2 | 3 | 4 | 5 | 6 | 7 | 8 | 9 | 10 |
|---|---|---|---|---|---|---|---|---|---|

I'm not convinced that the truth about God is something we can know for sure.

I'm unsure about what is true about God.

I'm convinced that the truth about God is something we can know for sure.

## Study It!

Take some time later this week to check out what the Bible teaches about the reliability of its Scriptures.

- ✦ Psalm 139:1–18
- ✦ Acts 17:24–31
- ✦ Romans 11:33–36
- ✦ 1 Corinthians 2:6–16

# Is
# Christianity
# Arrogant?

# Read It!

## Sound Advice?

There never seems to be a shortage of advice floating around. Everybody claims to have an expert opinion—and you wonder if any of them really know what in the world they're talking about. Take, for instance, the "words of wisdom" below. Which ones do you trust as absolutely true?

- Dr. Adams asked Rick to sit back down on the table so he could look at him at eye level. "Look, Mr. Jones, this is serious," he said. "I promise you that if you maintain a healthy, balanced diet, get plenty of rest, and exercise rigorously at least thirty minutes three times a week you'll feel like a new man. In fact, Mr. Jones, it's *the only right way* to lose weight and stay healthy."

- "Growing up, my mom always told me, 'An apple a day keeps the doctor away,' and you know what?" Tammy professed. "I've done exactly that. I eat at least one apple every day, and I'm never sick—never. It's *the key* to staying healthy."

- The oral hygienist held open Sally's mouth with one tool while she used another tool to poke each tooth one by one. "Brushing after meals and flossing every night is *the only effective way* to remove plaque from your teeth, Sally," the hygienist warned. "Unless you do that, you'll *definitely* be in here getting a filling from Dr. Lambert."

- "*Never* go outside without sunscreen," Uncle Harry said as his nephews Tim and Clayton were heading out the door to the beach. "Look at this scar," he paused, pointing at his arm with a frown. "Melanoma, boys, melanoma. Don't mean to scare you, but you'll get melanoma *for sure* if you don't wear sunscreen."

- Dan finished reading a health article he found stowed in the seat pocket in front of him. It made his cross-country flight seem that much faster. He glanced back at the one sentence that particularly caught his eye. "To eliminate toxins from your body and flush your system clean, you *must* drink eight glasses of purified water a day." As the flight attendant passed, he promptly asked for a large bottle of Evian.

- Rebecca brought her new boyfriend over to meet her grandmother, and was pleased at how well things were going. She carried some dishes to the kitchen, where Grandma was scraping the plates. "So, Gram, what do you think?" Grandma looked at her soberly and answered, "Rebecca, you'll *never* catch him if you don't learn to cook. If I've said it once, I've said it a hundred times, the *surefire* way to a man's heart is through his stomach."

- Mike shook his head and clucked his tongue. "What is it?" Toby asked. "Am I doing something wrong?" Mike wiped the grease and oil off his hands with a rag. "Listen, Mr. Wilcox, you're going to ruin your car if you don't start changing your oil regularly. You know that, right? You've got to change it every three months or 3,000 miles—*no exceptions.* I'm just glad you had this tire problem so we could take care of your oil at the same time." He kept shaking his head in disbelief. "You've just got to change your oil. Otherwise your engine's not going to run like it should!"

- For the teacher training day, the principal invited a math specialist to give some coaching. "Kids learn math *best* using a no-nonsense, back-to-the-basics, drilling approach," the lecturer announced. The teachers scribbled notes, some nodding, some shaking their heads. "It's *the only way* to get those facts to stick in their heads," he continued. "Use those flash cards like they're going out of style. Whatever you do, you must drill, drill, drill."

- "How am I supposed to get Henry to stop screaming?" Janet pleaded with her friend Angela on the phone. "Time out," Angela answered. "Okay," Janet responded. "I'm waiting." "No," Angela explained, "I mean, the 'time out' method is the *only* effective form of discipline for misbehaving children. I read it last year in a parenting magazine and tried it with Billy, and I'm telling you, Janet, it works. You try it, and you'll have Henry quieted down in no time. It's the best way. It's the *only* way. I promise you."

- "Now that you're old enough to help with the yard work, son, let me tell you something," Billy's dad said, leaning in close. "The *only way* to mow a lawn is on the diagonal. Lines parallel to the sidewalk or squares are all signs of an amateur who doesn't understand turf. It's *got* to be on the diagonal."

- John was adamant. "Look here, Joe, the Bible is very clear on this point. There's *no other way*. You can't get around it. Read it for yourself." Joe quickly grabbed the Bible right out of his friend's hands. "Let me see that. 'Jesus answered, "'I am the way and the truth and the life,'" he read out loud. "Keep reading; don't stop there," John interjected. "Okay, okay, don't interrupt me," Joe stated harshly. "'*No one comes to the Father except through me.*'" Joe grew silent. "There it is, clear as day, " he admitted.

So how helpful is all this advice anyway? After a while, you begin to catch on that most of it is simple exaggeration. Everybody means well, of course. When it comes right down to it, though, there's seldom just one way. To claim otherwise is arrogance, plain and simple. After all, there's always more than one way to skin a cat.

# Watch It!

Use the following space to take notes as you view the video in which Lee Strobel interviews Rick Warren, author of the best-selling book *The Purpose-Driven Life* and pastor of Saddleback Church in Lake Forest, California, one of the largest congregations in the country. *Time* magazine has called him "America's pastor."

## Discuss It!

**1** Rick Warren believes that our will, not God's, is done most of the time in this world. What does he mean by this? Do you agree or disagree?

**2** Where was God on September 11, 2001? Explain your answer. Rick Warren believes on that day God was in the hearts of the people who believe in him. Do you agree or disagree?

**3** Do believe what happened on September 11, 2001 was in accordance with God's will? Explain your answer.

**4** Do you agree with Rick Warren that the enormous outpouring of generosity and unselfishness following September 11, 2001 showed God in a thousand ways? Why or why not?

**5** Rick Warren believes that the answer to the question, "Why does God allow evil and suffering?" is our greatest curse and greatest blessing at the same time: that God has given each of us a free moral will and we make our own choices every day. Give examples of how free choice is a blessing and how it is a curse. Is free choice more of a curse than a blessing or vice versa? Explain.

**6** Does the fact that God gave us a free moral will justify the fact that evil and suffering are in our world?

**7** Rick Warren says, "God could have created us all like puppets where he pulls our strings and we pray several times a day and we always do the right thing, but God wanted a race of tested individuals who love him by choice." Do you agree that real love couldn't exist if we were God's programmed robots? Why or why not? What is the significance of love by choice?

**8** If heaven is a place where God's will is *always* done perfectly, does that mean that in heaven people will become God's puppets without free choice? Explain.

# Watch It!

Use the following space to take notes as Lee Strobel continues to interview Rick Warren.

## Discuss It!

**9** Rick Warren believes that "God does not grade on a curve. God has one standard and that is perfection." He further claims that heaven is a perfect place requiring nothing less than perfection from those who wish to enter. How are your beliefs similar to or different from Warren's? If Mother Teresa gets an "A" on her moral conduct report card, what's your grade?

**10** Is Christianity unfair? According to Christian belief, the Son of Sam who murdered several innocent people and yet became a Christian in prison is going to heaven, but the Dalai Lama, who isn't a Christian and yet helped all kinds of people his whole life, isn't going to spend eternity with God. Isn't that unfair? Explain your answers.

**11** Rick Warren's response to the Son of Sam/Dalai Lama dilemma is: if we're *all* on the sinking Titanic together, we *all* need a savior no matter how good or bad we are. According to the following Bible verses, in what ways are we *all* on a ship that's going down?

> The soul who sins is the one who will die.... But if a righteous man turns from his righteousness and commits sin and does the same detestable things the wicked man does, will he live? None of the righteous things he has done will be remembered. Because of the unfaithfulness he is guilty of and because of the sins he has committed, he will die. (Ezekiel 18:20, 24)

> But your iniquities have separated you from your God; your sins have hidden his face from you, so that he will not hear. (Isaiah 59:2)

> O LORD, God ... Here we are before you in our guilt, though because of it not one of us can stand in your presence. (Ezra 9:15)

> As it is written: "There is no one righteous, not even one." (Romans 3:10)

> "This is the verdict: Light has come into the world, but men loved darkness instead of light because their deeds were evil." (John 3:19)

> "I am absolutely against any religion that says that one faith is superior to another. I don't see how that is anything different than spiritual racism. It's a way of saying that we are closer to God than you, and that's what leads to hatred."
>
> **Rabbi Schmuley Boteach**

***12*** Do you agree that we *all* need a savior or do you think some people in this world are "good enough" to save themselves on their own? Explain.

***13*** What do you think is the destiny of people who haven't always done everything perfectly according to God's will? Explain.

**14** Rick Warren points out that if heaven is a perfect place, then only perfect people get in. And, since he's not perfect, he needs somebody else to buy his ticket. According to the following Bible verses, who holds the "ticket" to heaven?

> And this is the testimony: God has given us eternal life, and this life is in his Son. He who has the Son has life; he who does not have the Son of God does not have life. (1 John 5:11–12)

> "Enter through the narrow gate. For wide is the gate and broad is the road that leads to destruction, and many enter through it. But small is the gate and narrow the road that leads to life, and only a few find it." (Matthew 7:13–14)

> Therefore Jesus said again, "I tell you the truth, I am the gate ... whoever enters through me will be saved." (John 10:7, 9)

**15** If Jesus really is the Son of God, is it arrogant for him to claim that he is the *only* way to heaven? Explain your answer.

> "[Jesus said,] 'You know the way to the place where I am going.' Thomas said to him, 'Lord, we don't know where you are going, so how can we know the way?' Jesus answered, 'I am the way and the truth and the life. No one comes to the Father except through me. If you really knew me, you would know my Father as well. From now on, you do know him and have seen him.'"
>
> **John 14:4–7**

**16** Rick Warren says he's betting his life on a verse in the Bible which reads, "Jesus said, 'No one comes to the Father but by me.'" Which of the following are you betting your life and eternity on?

❏ I am basically a good person.
❏ I do the best I can.
❏ I'm involved in good causes.
❏ I do good deeds.
❏ I was baptized.
❏ I believe and trust in God.
❏ I believe and trust in Jesus.
❏ I attend church services.
❏ I am a member of a good church.
❏ I am a part of a Christian family.
❏ I'm betting there is nothing after this life.
❏ I'll find out when I get there.
❏ I believe in good karma and reincarnation.
❏ Other _____

## What about Those Who've Never Heard?

If Jesus claimed to be the only way to heaven, then what about those who have never heard of him?

Frankly, we don't have a complete answer. However, the Bible does tell us some things to help us sort through the issue.

First, we know from the Bible that everyone has a moral standard written on their hearts by God and that everybody is guilty of violating that standard. That's why our conscience bothers us when we do something wrong.

Second, we know that everyone has enough information from observing the created world to know that God exists, but people have suppressed that information and rejected God anyway—for which they rightfully deserve punishment.

Third, we know from both the Old and New Testaments that those who seek God will find him. In fact, the Bible says the Holy Spirit is seeking us first, making it possible for us to seek God.

This suggests that people who respond to the understanding that they have and who earnestly seek after the one true God will find an opportunity, in some way, to receive the eternal life that God has graciously provided through Jesus Christ. That could happen in a variety of ways. For instance, God could send a Christian to tell that person about Jesus, or he could reveal himself through a dream.

Repeatedly we see in Scripture that God is scrupulously fair. "Will not the Judge of all the earth do right?" asks Genesis 18:25. Says Ron Nash, author of *Is Jesus the Only Savior?*: "When God is finished dealing with all of us, none will be able to complain that they were treated unfairly."

Finally, we know that apart from the payment that Christ made on the cross, nobody has a chance of getting off spiritual death row. Exactly how much knowledge a person has to have about Jesus or precisely where the lines of faith are drawn, only God knows. He and he alone can expose the motives of a person's heart.

As for you and me, the issue isn't ignorance. We've heard the message of Jesus. It's clear that we're responsible for how we respond.

It's like the story about comedian W. C. Fields anxiously flipping through a Bible while on his deathbed. When asked what he was doing, Fields replied, "Looking for loopholes, m'boy, looking for loopholes."

Let me tell you: I've looked. They're not there.

*Lee Strobel*

## Watch It! *Lee's Perspective*

When people say Christianity is arrogant for claiming Jesus is the only way to God, I like to ask them to imagine two country clubs. The first has a strict set of rules and only allows in people who have earned their membership. They have to accomplish something, obtain superior wisdom, or fulfill a long list of demands and requirements to quality for entry. Despite their best efforts, lots of people just won't make the grade and will be excluded.

In effect, this is what every other religious system is like. All faiths, except Christianity, are based on the "Do Plan." That is, they involve people *doing* something, through their struggling and striving, to somehow try to earn the good favor of God. Adherents must go on a pilgrimage, give alms to the poor, perform good deeds, chant the right words, go through a series of reincarnations, or faithfully follow some other religious drill.

But the other country club is different. It throws its doors wide open and says, "Anyone who wants membership is invited inside. Rich or poor, black or white, regardless of your ethnic heritage or where you live, we would love to include you. Entry is based not on your qualifications but only on accepting this free invitation, because Jesus has already paid the price of admission. So we'll leave the matter to you. You decide. But remember — we will never turn you away if you seek admittance."

That's what Christianity is like. It's based on the "Done Plan," or what Jesus has *done* for us on the cross. The Bible teaches that we're all spiritual rebels and that nobody can *do* anything to merit heaven. But Jesus died as our substitute on the cross and is offering forgiveness and eternal life as a free gift of his grace.

So which country club is being snobbish?

Other religious leaders can offer pithy and helpful insights, but only Jesus—because he is the unique and perfect Son of God—is qualified to offer himself as payment for our wrongdoing. No leader of any other major religion even pretends to be able to do that.

Said theologian R.C. Sproul: "Moses could mediate on the law; Muhammad could brandish a sword; Buddha could give personal counsel; Confucius could offer wise sayings. But none of these men was qualified to offer an atonement for the sins of the world."

## Chart It!

At this point in your spiritual journey, what do you believe about the apparent arrogance behind the claims of Christianity? On a scale from one to ten, place an X near the spot and phrase that best describes you. Share your selection with the rest of the group and give reasons for placing your X where you did.

| 1 | 2 | 3 | 4 | 5 | 6 | 7 | 8 | 9 | 10 |
|---|---|---|---|---|---|---|---|---|---|
| I'm convinced that Christianity is arrogant. | | | | I'm unsure about whether Christianity is arrogant. | | | | I'm convinced that Christianity is not arrogant. | |

## Study It!

Take some time later this week to check out what the Bible teaches about Christian beliefs.

✦ John 3
✦ Romans 3
✦ Ephesians 2

*If you want to go deeper into the topics Lee introduced, get the complete story.*

# The Case for Christ
*A Journalist's Personal Investigation of the Evidence for Jesus*

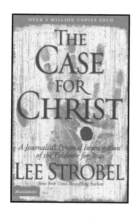

Is Jesus really the divine Son of God? What reason is there to believe that he is?

In his bestseller *The Case for Christ*, the legally trained investigative reporter Lee Strobel examined the claims of Christ by retracing his own spiritual journey, reaching the hard-won yet satisfying verdict that Jesus is God's unique son.

Written in the style of a blockbuster investigative report, *The Case for Christ* consults a dozen authorities on Jesus with doctorates from Cambridge, Princeton, Brandeis, and other top-flight institutions to present:

- Historical evidence
- Psychiatric evidence
- Other evidence
- Scientific evidence
- Fingerprint evidence

This colorful, hard-hitting book is no novel. It's a riveting quest for the truth about history's most compelling figure.

"Lee Strobel asks the questions a tough-minded skeptic would ask. Every inquirer should have it."

—*Phillip E. Johnson, law professor, University of California at Berkeley*

Hardcover 0-310-22646-5
Softcover 0-310-20930-7
Evangelism Pack 0-310-22605-8
Mass Market 6-pack 0-310-22627-9
Audio Pages® Abridged Cassette 0-310-24824-8
Audio Pages® Unabridged Cassette 0-310-21960-4
Audio Pages® Unabridged CD 0-310-24779-9

# The Case for Faith

*A Journalist Investigates
the Toughest Objections to
Christianity*

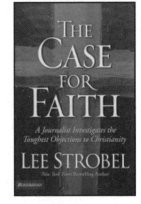

In his best-seller *The Case for Christ*, Lee
Strobel examined the claims of Christ,
reaching the hard-won yet satisfying verdict that Jesus is God's unique son.

But despite the compelling historical
evidence that Strobel presented, many grapple with doubts or
serious concerns about faith in God. As in a court of law, they
want to shout, "Objection!" They say, "If God is love, then
what about all of the suffering that festers in our world?" Or,
"If Jesus is the door to heaven, then what about the millions
who have never heard of him?"

In *The Case for Faith*, Strobel turns his tenacious investigative skills to the most persistent emotional objections to belief,
the eight "heart" barriers to faith. *The Case for Faith* is for
those who may be feeling attracted toward Jesus, but who are
faced with formidable intellectual barriers standing squarely in
their path. For Christians, it will deepen their convictions and
give them fresh confidence in discussing Christianity with even
their most skeptical friends.

Hardcover 0-310-22015-7
Softcover 0-310-23469-7
Evangelism Pack 0-310-23508-1
Mass Market 6-pack 0-310-23509X
Audio Pages® Abridged Cassettes 0-310-23475-1

*Pick up a copy today at your favorite bookstore!*

**GRAND RAPIDS, MICHIGAN 49530 USA**

WWW.ZONDERVAN.COM

> *"My road to atheism was paved by science . . . . But, ironically, so was my later journey to God."*—Lee Strobel

# The Case for a Creator:
### *A Journalist Investigates Scientific Evidence That Points Toward God*

*Lee Strobel, Author of*
The Case for Christ *and*
The Case for Faith

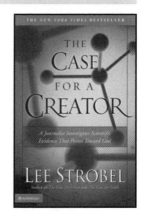

During his academic years, Lee Strobel became convinced that God was outmoded, a belief that colored his ensuing career as an award-winning journalist at the *Chicago Tribune*. Science had made the idea of a Creator irrelevant—or so Strobel thought.

But today science is pointing in a different direction. In recent years, a diverse and impressive body of research has increasingly supported the conclusion that the universe was intelligently designed. At the same time, Darwinism has faltered in the face of concrete facts and hard reason.

Has science discovered God? At the very least, it's giving faith an immense boost as new findings emerge about the incredible complexity of our universe. Join Strobel as he reexamines the theories that once led him away from God. Through his compelling and highly readable account, you'll encounter the mind-stretching discoveries from cosmology, cellular biology, DNA research, astronomy, physics, and human consciousness that present astonishing evidence in *The Case for a Creator.*

Hardcover: 0-310-24144-8
Unabridged Audio Pages® CD: 0-310-25439-6

ebooks:
Adobe Acrobat eBook Reader®: 0-310-25977-0
Microsoft Reader®: 0-310-25978-9
Palm™ Edition: 0-310-25979-7
Unabridged ebook Download: 0-310-26142-2

# The Case for Easter
## *A Journalist Investigates the Evidence for the Resurrection*

### *Lee Strobel*

*Did Jesus of Nazareth really rise from the dead?*

Of the many world religions, only one claims that its founder returned from the grave. The resurrection of Jesus Christ is the very cornerstone of Christianity.

But a dead man coming back to life? In our sophisticated age, when myth has given way to science, who can take such a claim seriously? Some argue that Jesus never died on the cross. Conflicting accounts make the empty tomb seem suspect. And post-crucifixion sightings of Jesus have been explained in psychological terms.

How credible is the evidence for—and against—the resurrection? Focusing his award-winning skills as a legal journalist on history's most compelling enigma, Lee Strobel retraces the startling findings that led him from atheism to belief. Drawing on expert testimony first shared in his blockbuster book *The Case for Christ,* Strobel examines:

The Medical Evidence—Was Jesus' death a sham and his resurrection a hoax?

The Evidence of the Missing Body—Was Jesus' body really absent from his tomb?

The Evidence of Appearances—Was Jesus seen alive after his death on the cross?

Written in a hard-hitting journalistic style, *The Case for Easter* probes the core issues of the resurrection. Jesus Christ, risen from the dead: superstitious myth or life-changing reality? The evidence is in. The verdict is up to you.

Mass Market: 0-310-25475-2

# The Case for Christmas
## A *Journalist Investigates the Identity of the Child in the Manger*

*Lee Strobel*

*Who was in the manger that first Christmas morning?*

Some say he would become a great moral leader. Others, a social critic. Still others view Jesus as a profound philosopher, a rabbi, a feminist, a prophet, and more. Many are convinced he was the divine Son of God.

Who was he—really? And how can you know for sure?

Consulting experts on the Bible, archaeology, and messianic prophecy, Lee Strobel searches out the true identity of the child in the manger. Join him as he asks the tough, pointed questions you'd expect from an award-winning legal journalist. If Jesus really was God in the flesh, then there ought to be credible evidence, including

Eyewitness Evidence—Can the biographies of Jesus be trusted?

Scientific Evidence—What does archaeology reveal?

Profile Evidence—Did Jesus fulfill the attributes of God?

Fingerprint Evidence—Did Jesus uniquely match the identity of the Messiah?

*The Case for Christmas* invites you to consider why Christmas matters in the first place. Somewhere beyond the traditions of the holiday lies the truth. It may be more compelling than you've realized. Weigh the facts ... and decide for yourself.

Jacketed Hardcover: 0-310-26629-7

# The Case for Faith
# Visual Edition

*Lee Strobel*

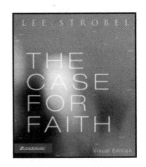

Open this book and open your eyes. It is
unlike any other you have held; a visual
feast for your eyes and a spiritual feast for
your soul. Lee Strobel, former atheist and award-winning legal
editor of the *Chicago Tribune,* asks hard questions about God
in *The Case for Faith* Visual Edition. And then he explores them
with evidence from archaeology, history, and science—all set in
powerful imagery and stunning typography. See the evidence for
faith as you've never seen it before.

Softcover: 0-310-25906-1

*Pick up a copy today at your favorite bookstore!*

**ZONDERVAN**™

**GRAND RAPIDS, MICHIGAN 49530 USA**
WWW.ZONDERVAN.COM

# God's Outrageous Claims
*Discover What They Mean for You*

## *Lee Strobel*

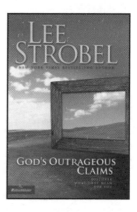

Lee Strobel presents thirteen phenomenal claims by God that can change the entire trajectory of your life and revolutionize your attitude, your character, and your relationships.

Take the Bible seriously and you'll discover that God makes some pretty amazing claims about you—and about what he wants to do in your life. *God's Outrageous Claims* examines important assertions that can transform your life into an adventure of faith, growth, and lasting fulfillment.

Discover how to grow in virtue, relate to others with authenticity, and make a real difference. *God's Outrageous Claims* is your guide to an exciting and challenging spiritual journey that can change you and your world profoundly.

Jacketed Hardcover: 0-310-26612-2

*Pick up a copy today at your favorite bookstore!*

**ZONDERVAN**™

GRAND RAPIDS, MICHIGAN 49530 USA

WWW.ZONDERVAN.COM

# Tough Questions

*Garry Poole and Judson Poling*

"The profound insights and candor captured in these guides will sharpen your mind, soften your heart, and inspire you and the members of your group to find vital answers together."

—Bill Hybels

This second edition of Tough Questions, designed for use in any small group setting, is ideal for use in seeker small groups. Based on more than five years of field-tested feedback, extensive revisions make this best-selling series easier to use and more appealing than ever for both participants and group leaders.

Softcover

How Does Anyone Know God Exists? ISBN 0-310-24502-8

What Difference Does Jesus Make? ISBN 0-310-24503-6

How Reliable Is the Bible? ISBN 0-310-24504-4

How Could God Allow Suffering and Evil? ISBN 0-310-24505-2

Don't All Religions Lead to God? ISBN 0-310-24506-0

Do Science and the Bible Conflict? ISBN 0-310-24507-9

Why Become a Christian? ISBN 0-310-24508-7

Leader's Guide ISBN 0-310-24509-5

We want to hear from you. Please send your comments about this book to us in care of zreview@zondervan.com. Thank you.

GRAND RAPIDS, MICHIGAN 49530 USA

ZONDERVAN.COM/
AUTHOR**TRACKER**